Why Do We Need Both Liquidity Regulations and a Lender of Last Resort? A Perspective from Federal Reserve Lending during the 2007-09 U.S. Financial Crisis

1.   Introduction

The 2007–09 financial crisis highlighted both the vulnerability of the financial system to liquidity shocks and the associated role of central bank lending.[1] In particular, the crisis was characterized by severe disruptions to the money markets where banks and other financial institutions acquire short-term funding. As institutions became unwilling to lend to each other, the cost of borrowing in short-term funding markets, as indicated by the spread between Libor and overnight index swaps (OIS), rose to unprecedented levels and the flow of credit in financial markets became severely disrupted (Figure 1).[2] To replace the funding normally provided in these markets and thereby keep credit flowing to U.S. businesses and households, the Federal Reserve responded by using a mix of traditional and less traditional policy tools, including emergency liquidity facilities. The amount of credit outstanding provided by the Federal Reserve to support the financial system peaked in December 2008 at over $1.5 trillion (Figure 2).

The scale of Federal Reserve intervention in financial markets during the crisis generated considerable controversy, and U.S. lawmakers and regulators subsequently took various steps to reduce the chances of a future financial crisis and to reduce the likelihood that lending by the Federal Reserve would be required in the future even if there were a financial crisis. For example, as part of the Basel III liquidity and capital rules, liquidity regulations were implemented that require banks to maintain more liquid balance sheets. Additionally, to prevent Federal Reserve loans from being used to support failing institutions, the authority of the Federal Reserve to provide emergency liquidity to individual nonbank institutions was eliminated.

Part of the motivation for these regulatory and legal changes was the view that central bank lending was itself a bad thing—that the loans were bailouts of financial institutions that protected them from the consequences of their risky behavior. Within the economic literature, moral hazard is seen as the principle cost associated with central bank lending as it encourages

---

[1] In this paper, we focus on emergency lending assistance by the central bank as opposed to more routine, daily lending operations. In the vast majority of cases, normal discount window loans are extended simply to cover end-of-day overdrafts or to equilibrate supply and demand in the market for reserve balances.
[2] Libor is the rate banks report being able to borrow on a short-term basis in the London interbank market. OIS represents the average overnight rate expected to prevail in markets targeted by central banks. The spread represents both credit risk of the underlying institutions and a cost of liquidity for lending funds at term, albeit short-term.

institutions to take on more risk than they would otherwise.[3] Some have also criticized this lending on the grounds that it pushed central bank policy into fiscal policy and threatened the independence of the Federal Reserve.[4] These concerns have led to proposals by some to eliminate even the remaining emergency authority of the Federal Reserve to lend in "unusual and exigent circumstances."[5]

A contrary view starts with the observation that the recent financial crisis involved massive disruptions to money markets and loss of liquidity across many financial markets, and thus significant negative consequences for the real economy. In this framework, the loss of liquidity is the result of a market failure, and if the central bank can solve that failure by lending, the result should be an unambiguous social good. After all, central banks are designed to create liquidity and, in the spirit of the classical doctrine of the LOLR (Bagehot, 1873), they should respond forcefully in a crisis. Former Federal Reserve Chairman Ben Bernanke described the crisis lending as nothing new and noted that "We did what central banks have done for many years and what they were designed to do: We served as a source of liquidity and stability in financial markets, and, in the broader economy, we worked to foster economic recovery and price stability."[6] Moreover, in the recent crisis, despite a massive loan book that included loans to institutions well outside its traditional network of depository institutions, the Federal Reserve had zero defaults or even delinquencies on those loans even though the crisis proceeded in several increasingly severe waves. While it is never possible to know what could have happened if the situation had worsened further, that all these loans were repaid underscores the important role of liquidity in driving the crisis and raises the question of why liquidity regulations are necessary at all as long as there are sufficiently robust capital requirements.

In this paper, we argue that the disparate views on the need for liquidity regulations and the role of LOLR arise because, in extremis, financial institutions experience a liquidity shortfall

---

[3] See Stern and Feldman (2004) and Freixas et al. (1999) for a detailed discussion and a summary of the related literature.

[4] See Goodfriend (2011) as an example.

[5] See Jeffrey Lacker (2013), "Lacker Testifies on Bankruptcy and Financial Institution Insolvency," testimony before the Subcommittee on Regulatory Reform, Commercial and Antitrust Law of the Committee on the Judiciary, December 3, www.richmondfed.org/press_room/speeches/president_jeff_lacker/2013/lacker_testimony_20131203.cfm.

[6] See Bernanke, Ben (2013), "Opening Remarks," speech delivered at the Ceremony Commemorating the Centennial of the Federal Reserve Act, Washington, December 16, www.federalreserve.gov/newsevents/speech/bernanke20131216a.htm.

because they are in one of two different types of situations that, in turn, have different implications for central bank lending. In particular, while liquidity provision by financial intermediaries is socially valuable, it exposes them to two types of situations where, in the absence of central bank intervention, they will be forced to fire-sell illiquid assets or, in a more severe case, fail altogether; both outcomes imply significant negative externalities to other financial institutions and the broader economy. First, sound institutions can face runs or a deterioration in the liquidity of markets they depend upon for funding. These marketwide, "pure liquidity" situations can be well addressed by a LOLR with minimal cost and no moral hazard, and liquidity regulations seem unnecessary. Second, solvency concerns can cause creditors to pull away from troubled institutions. Since LOLR lending in these situations cannot be extended in a way that reliably eliminates or correctly prices for credit risk, it is rife with moral hazard and therefore best avoided if at all possible by having robust liquidity and capital regulations and means to resolve the institution in an orderly way.

Of course, in reality, liquidity shortfalls often include elements of both situations.[7] However, presenting these two extremes is valuable for illustrating many of the issues involved with LOLR lending. To shed light on these issues, our analysis reviews examples of Federal Reserve lending during the crisis, in which both types of liquidity situations figured prominently. Based on these observations, we contend that liquidity regulations, combined with other regulatory tools, are an important complement to the LOLR and are particularly valuable in mitigating the moral hazard concerns that arise with the existence of a LOLR. Our discussion also points to when it is appropriate to use the LOLR and when to use the liquidity buffers mandated by the liquidity regulations.

More specifically, we argue that, first, liquidity or other regulations do not make a LOLR unnecessary—lending forcefully by the LOLR during times of systemic shocks is an important element of optimal policy. Requiring banks to hold high enough liquidity buffers to meet liquidity demands associated with a systemic crisis would lead to less than socially optimal levels of liquidity and maturity transformation. More importantly, during stress episodes, as

---

[7] This approach is also a shortcut where we implicitly assume that these two situations are somewhat of a proxy for whether the problem can be reasonably attributed to the bank's own decisions or to a completely exogenous shock. In other words, we are silent with respective to potential collective moral hazard, highlighted, for example, in Farhi and Tirole (2012).

banks subject to various liquidity shocks become unable to fulfill their obligations in a timely fashion or become concerned about their ability to do so, they would seek to hold larger liquidity buffers and not lend the funds out, exacerbating the liquidity shortage. Such dynamics were a part of the panics that led to the creation of the Federal Reserve (Sprague, 1913; Carlson, 2013). If banks are confident that they can borrow from the central bank to meet any unforeseen liquidity needs, then they would not pull back from lending even amid increased uncertainty about future liquidity needs.

On the other hand, liquidity regulations and other policy tools, such as an orderly resolution authority, are needed to mitigate the potential costs (including moral hazard) and limits of LOLR lending and increase the likelihood that when central bank lending does occur, it is in response to marketwide, pure liquidity situations. In particular, liquidity regulations are valuable in two ways. First, they serve as a tax on liquidity risk by requiring banks to hold low-yielding assets in rough proportion to the amount of liquidity risk they take. As such, they provide an incentive for banks to internalize the externalities associated with liquidity crises, at least to some extent, and accordingly minimize their occurrence. Second, in the event a liquidity situation emerges, it is often difficult for the central bank to quickly determine the nature of the situation. The central bank needs time to make the determination while the supervisory authority is simultaneously preparing for possible orderly resolution. In those cases, liquidity regulations in conjunction with supervisory oversight would help ensure that the central bank and other prudential authorities have the necessary time to assess the nature of the shortfall and arrange the appropriate response, if any is needed. Similarly, it is important to establish sufficiently low-cost resolution regimes to reduce the cost of allowing an institution to fail when its illiquidity is the consequence of solvency rather than liquidity concerns. While central banks can to some extent control the potential moral hazard associated with lending by pricing credit risk correctly or, more practically, by driving credit risk to zero by taking a large amount of collateral, this approach may actually hinder their ability to address liquidity troubles at times as we discuss in detail below.

Finally, while the above reasoning suggests a role for both a LOLR and liquidity regulations, it does not suggest that the appropriate arrangement is that a financial institution should first run down its liquidity reserves and only then borrow; that is, we do not subscribe to the view that liquidity regulations are intended to ensure that central banks should be the lender of *last*—and not *first*—resort. If the situation giving rise to the liquidity need is related to concerns about the bank's solvency, then the central bank should not lend at all because of the associated credit risk and moral hazard. Instead, the liquidity buffer should be used to gain sufficient time to arrange an orderly resolution (by the institution itself or the authorities) to the underlying problem. But if the situation is marketwide, then the LOLR should immediately provide liquidity broadly so that financial institutions do not need to run down their liquidity buffers. In this situation, central bank lending should enable banks to maintain their liquidity reserves to meet potential idiosyncratic stress and build confidence in the system.

A look at both the Federal Reserve's own lending history and the literature on the LOLR reveals that disagreements about the nature and purpose of central bank lending run deep and have a long history. For example, Friedman and Schwartz (1963) provide a detailed discussion of a similar divide within the Federal Reserve in the late 1920s as the policymakers debate whether they could restrain "speculative," "undesirable" credit while maintaining a preferential treatment for "legitimate" borrowing. The Board of Governors of the Federal Reserve (1971, p. 6) reviews the evolution of the discount window and notes that, at times, regulations were set to "reinforce a policy of limited bank use of the discount window" buttressed by "disciplinary contacts by discount officers." These policies, as noted more recently by Gorton and Metrick (2013, p. 52), "complicated lender-of-last-resort policy ever since." The shifts in the debate about the "appropriate" use of the discount window have swung between concerns about too much lending (for example, in the 1950s and 1980s) and too little lending (for example, in the late 1960s and 2000s).

The literature on the LOLR similarly provides a long range of these alternative views, which are well summarized in Freixas et al. (1999) and Bordo (1990). The classical position, often attributed to Bagehot (1873) and Thornton (1802), is that the LOLR should provide funding freely to illiquid but solvent institutions against high-quality collateral and at a penalty rate to allay a panic. However, the literature is full of papers pointing to the difficulties of distinguishing between liquidity and solvency problems, especially during a crisis, as well as the potential problems with how to define and impose a penalty rate (see, for instance, Goodhart, 1999). These issues lead, on the one extreme, to the view that the Federal Reserve should only provide liquidity to the market as a whole via open market operations, but not to individual banks, since liquidity would then be allocated to individual, creditworthy banks via the interbank market (see Goodfriend and King, 1988; Bordo, 1990; and Schwartz, 1992 and 1995). On the other extreme is the view that the LOLR will have to assist illiquid and insolvent institutions at times, and that lending should not be at a penalty rate because the elevated rate could worsen the problems of a bank receiving support (see Goodhart, 1985 and 1987; Goodhart and Schoenmaker, 1995). The literature also has a long discussion of the moral hazard consequences as a cost that offsets the benefit of central bank lending as noted in Freixas et al. (1999), though there is also a range of perspectives that point out that the collapse of liquidity is a market failure and the central bank provision of liquidity is a public good. For instance, Holmstrom and Tirole (1998) note that public insurance against aggregate risks should allow firms to undertake more profitable activities with higher social return. Others note that there is no moral hazard as long as central banks provide the liquidity against properly priced collateral (for example, Buiter, 2007) or that moral hazard can be managed by various policies, such as constructive ambiguity (for example, Freixas, 1999) and regulations (for example, Cao and Illing, 2011).

Our paper's main contribution to the literature is to reconcile these different perspectives by thinking of central bank lending as encompassing two very different types of liquidity demands and using that as a guide to think about the right mix of LOLR and regulatory tools. Moreover, our discussion on the Federal Reserve's experience during the crisis also illustrates some of the key real-time issues faced by a LOLR that arise during a crisis and the associated limitations of a LOLR as a policy tool.

The remainder of the paper proceeds as follows. In the next section, we describe in more detail the liquidity situations in which either a LOLR or liquidity regulations—but not both—are desirable. In the third section, we provide an analysis of the Federal Reserve's lending during the financial crisis to further highlight the two types of liquidity situations. In the fourth section, we present our views on optimal regulatory and lending policy. In the fifth section, we provide our conclusions.

2.   Two liquidity situations and two polar views of lending versus regulation

Banks have fairly illiquid assets funded with runnable liabilities. We take as a given that such liquidity transformation is socially valuable. In particular, funding loans with short-term liabilities, such as demand deposits, is a relatively efficient arrangement as the latter are safe, easy-to-value claims that create a flow of money-like benefits for their holders.[8] However, as a result, banks are vulnerable to a withdrawal of funding. In this section, we describe two types of liquidity situations in which such funding demands may arise with different implications for whether the optimal policy response is ex post central bank lending or ex ante liquidity regulations. In the first situation, liquidity demands are associated with broad-based, run-like situations on solvent institutions or a deterioration in the markets these institutions rely on for liquidity. These cases are behind the view that central bank lending is the right response to liquidity needs and ex ante liquidity regulations are an unnecessary tax. In the second situation, liquidity needs are those of an individual institution and are associated with concerns about the institution's solvency and potential disorderly failure. These cases, in turn, underlie the view that liquidity and other regulations should at least be the first line of defense and that a LOLR is problematic.

2.1 When is LOLR the best solution and liquidity regulations an unnecessary tax?

The theoretical and historical literature identify several mechanisms through which solvent banks may experience liquidity problems owing to a marketwide stress that are exogenous from the viewpoint of an individual institution. In a relatively simple example, liquidity shocks could arise in the form of "sunspot" bank runs as first modeled by Diamond and Dybvig (1983), where depositors may run due to coordination problems despite certainty about the soundness of a bank. In a more detailed setting, the network structure of interbank claims may mean that the failure of one bank could result in liquidity crunches at other, otherwise sound institutions (Allen and Gale, 2007; Riksbank, 2003). There are also examples where shocks to alternative funding markets, such as the commercial paper market, can rapidly increase the demand for bank funding or draws on lines of credit that in turn cause banks to experience a liquidity crunch (Calomiris, 1994). Typically, banks can rely on the interbank market to meet funding shortfalls. However,

---

[8] See Kashyap et al. (2002), Gorton and Pennacchi (1990), Diamond and Dybvig (1983), and Holmstrom and Tirole (1998).

this market may be unable to meet these needs if there is an aggregate shortfall in the availability of reserves or if some of the inherent imperfections in this market are exacerbated during stress periods.[9] Liquidity in this market may also dry up if banks refuse to lend because they are not confident that they will be able to borrow in the interbank market themselves should they need liquidity down the road.

A LOLR is the preferred solution to address these types of marketwide, pure liquidity situations. By lending against illiquid assets that would otherwise be fire-sold, the central bank can provide liquidity to the affected institutions at a minimal cost to itself. There is no moral hazard as liquidity needs owe to an exogenous marketwide stress, and there is either no credit risk or the central bank can price any credit risk it incurs perfectly. A liquidity regulation beyond capital requirements that would make the banks hold enough cash to deal with the risk of such situations would lead to less than socially optimal liquidity and maturity transformation and therefore be a costly, unnecessary tax.

Moreover, central bank lending is the only solution in these circumstances that prevents self-reinforcing liquidity spirals, costly defaults, and a large contraction of credit to the real economy. Absent the availability of such lending, a shock that causes demand for liquid assets to exceed available supply would be exacerbated during stress episodes if banks sought to hold even larger liquidity buffers and were unwilling to lend them out due to concerns about their ability to obtain funding in the event they experienced such a shock. Such dynamics were a part of the panics that led to the creation of the Federal Reserve (Sprague, 1913; Carlson, 2013). If banks are confident that they can borrow from the central bank to meet any unforeseen funding needs, then they would not pull back from lending even amid increased uncertainty about future funding needs.

In fact, in much of the economics literature, a LOLR is seen as the primary method for dealing with these types of liquidity problems and run-like situations. For example, in Diamond and Dybvig (1983), just the presence of the LOLR, without any lending, can eliminate run-risk altogether, increasing social welfare at zero cost. Similarly, Holmstrom and Tirole (1998) show that public provision of liquidity in the presence of aggregate shocks is a pure public good, with

---

[9] See, for example, Rochet and Tirole (1996) and Acharya et al. (2012). See Carlson and Wheelock (2012) for historical examples of deteriorations in funding markets during stress episodes.

no moral hazard involved. Lending by the central bank also helps contain potential effects on the financial system of the failure of illiquid but solvent banks, which would involve significant negative externalities.

Several key assumptions underlie this view. The first is that the institution is fundamentally solvent. The second is that the liquidity needs are exogenous and do not arise because of a change in the creditworthiness of the institution. The third is that the LOLR is confident that both of these conditions are met. Additionally, the following are often (though not necessarily) assumed: the liquidity needs are modest relative to the unencumbered assets of the bank; the incentives to gamble for survival and shift risk to the deposit insurance fund are low because the institution is solvent; and the funding shocks will be brief. Because the liquidity need is unrelated to concerns about the balance sheet of the bank, the central bank is not subject to adverse selection. Accordingly, the central bank can indeed meet the liquidity needs by extending a loan without generating moral hazard, while at the same time pricing any credit risk correctly.

Put differently, in a world where credit risk is negligible or the central bank is confident that it can measure and price for the credit risk correctly, it is socially optimal for the central bank to backstop the entirety of liquidity risk because it is the only agent in the economy that is not exposed to liquidity risk. In such a world, the addition of liquidity regulations is not necessary at all, especially once a strong capital regulation is in place to ensure the solvency of institutions. In addition, requiring banks to hold liquid assets is an unnecessary tax because it only leads to a lower provision of liquidity services and lending without any clear benefits.

Of course, these are unrealistic assumptions. In the real world, liquidity and solvency are often closely linked, especially during stress episodes, and central banks cannot distinguish with certainty whether or not an institution is solvent. Relatedly, the central bank's ability to price credit risk is not necessarily better than that of other market participants, which is one reason, for example, why central banks tend to significantly overcollateralize their loans, especially because they are risk averse and permitted by the public to take only a small amount of risk. But such overcollateralization may actually hinder a central bank's ability to stop runs in certain situations. As we discuss in the next section, it is when these assumptions most clearly do not hold that liquidity regulations are most effective.

2.2 When is the use of LOLR problematic and liquidity regulation the best solution?

In contrast to the situations reviewed in the previous section, liquidity situations can also arise when the creditors of an institution pull back out of concern about the riskiness of the institution and its solvency. Such investor runs occur in part because short-term investors are, as a rule, extremely risk averse given the low margins associated with the investment and the high cost of dealing with a defaulted loan or reverse repurchase agreement. To be clear, what we have in mind are situations where the solvency of the institution is questionable and not that the institution is clearly insolvent. If the institution is insolvent, it should be closed.[10]

In these situations, there are significant costs associated with LOLR lending even as disorderly default imposes externalities on the rest of society. These costs are intrinsically related to the assumptions that underlie the cases in which a LOLR is the best solution, as described above. First, the optimality of the LOLR heavily depends on the institutions subject to the liquidity situation being solvent. But in real life, the line between illiquidity and insolvency is often blurry, and the central bank cannot always easily distinguish and disentangle risks (and is not necessarily wiser than the market). Consequently, lending in a crisis entails the LOLR taking more credit risk than it would in normal times. But central banks are often risk averse because taking on credit risk may be judged by the public as inappropriately engaging in credit allocation or providing subsidies to financial institutions, and society may judge that such actions should be undertaken by the fiscal authority, if at all. These concerns are likely to be particularly acute in situations when the potential borrower's liquidity need is the result of investor concerns about the borrower's assets and general financial condition.

Second, in these types of liquidity situations, LOLR lending is rife with moral hazard costs because the risk is not just related to liquidity but credit risk as well, and the central bank cannot necessarily price or eliminate this risk. Moral hazard concerns arise because financial institutions will be more willing to take on credit risk when they know that, should their solvency situation deteriorate, the LOLR will shield them from the costs typically associated with an impaired condition (that is, underprice its lending to the institutions). Further, while the financial institution will not take into account the externalities associated with illiquidity and default, the

---

[10] See Freixas et al. (2000) for a discussion of the need for a LOLR to act to preserve financial stability in situations in which a large financial institution may be insolvent.

central bank will take those costs into account when deciding whether to lend. In particular, the central bank will prefer to lend as long as the social benefit of avoiding the externalities exceeds the social cost of lending. The central bank will, therefore, be forced to take on more risk than it would prefer to avoid the social costs associated with a potentially avoidable liquidity default. Even more perniciously, short-term creditors of financial institutions will be aware that the central bank will lend, which will allow those creditors to be repaid even if the institution ultimately fails. As a result, short-term creditors will require minimal risk spreads. Financial institutions will therefore increase their reliance on short-term credit to maximize their profits and likely will take on more credit risk, increasing the frequency that the central bank will find it necessary to intervene.

While moral hazard and risk of losses could be mitigated to some extent by taking in conservatively priced collateral, there are significant limitations to this approach.[11] As evidenced by the crisis, in some circumstances it is counterproductive for the Federal Reserve to claim a large amount of collateral. If the Federal Reserve takes so much collateral that the risk to other short-term creditors goes up, then those creditors have an even greater incentive to run, which would exacerbate the situation. In addition, if Federal Reserve lending allows greater exit by uninsured depositors of a troubled bank, such lending could increase the resolution costs borne by remaining creditors or the FDIC Deposit Insurance Fund. Indeed, the Federal Deposit Insurance Corporation Improvement Act of 1991 (FDICIA) placed restrictions on discount window lending by the Federal Reserve to undercapitalized banks for this reason.

Similarly, constructive ambiguity does not appear to be a convincing solution to moral hazard because of time-inconsistency problems. Corrigan (1990), for example, argues that by introducing an element of uncertainty into the provision of support, pressure can, in principle, be maintained on banks to act prudently since each individual bank will not know whether it will be rescued. But, in each individual case, the central bank would always have an incentive to lend to avoid the social costs of default while promising not to lend in the future. Thus, a plan not to lend in these situations might not be time consistent. Moreover, even if there were simply some doubt about the central bank's ability to refrain from lending, market discipline of the potential

---

[11] Bindseil (2013) provides a model that shows how an overly protecting risk management approach with a lot of asset encumbrance limits the LOLR's ability to stabilize the markets.

borrower would be reduced, making the lending outcome even more likely. Besides, constructive ambiguity contradicts the classical view, as described in Bagehot (1873), which emphasizes the need to clarify the conditions for access to the LOLR in advance to all interested parties.

It is precisely because of these costs associated with the LOLR that liquidity regulations, combined in particular with an orderly resolution authority, may be the optimal solution to address these situations. It might even be appropriate to eliminate a LOLR rather than just expect the LOLR to simply decline to lend. During normal times, these regulations will compensate for the tendency for institutions to not take into account the externalities associated with liquidity crises and fire sale dynamics when deciding on the appropriate liquidity of their balance sheets. Put differently, these regulations will help limit liquidity risk in the system, in the sense that forcing banks to hold lower-yielding liquid assets in proportion to the riskiness of their liquidity profile is an implicit tax on liquidity provision. When liquidity troubles arise, these regulations will ensure that banks have liquidity buffers that they can use, which should lead to a better outcome. The buffers will allow time for a financial institution to continue making payments while it is working through a period of illiquidity or while a resolution is being arranged. To this latter point, the regulation would be especially effective if combined with an orderly resolution process as well as prompt and aggressive attention on the part of supervisors to a building liquidity shortfall.

Even though a regulatory response without a LOLR may be the best response to liquidity situations related to concerns about an individual institution's solvency, such a response does not help address another important liquidity dynamic—contagion. In particular, even if the initial liquidity shock may be driven by concerns about an institution's solvency, the failure or potential resolution of that institution may lead to runs on other banks, and a LOLR will be necessary to help limit the impact of such a contagion. In other words, given the nature of liquidity needs— whether idiosyncratic or system-wide—the best solution will necessarily entail both LOLR and liquidity regulation, as discussed in more detail in section 4. But first, in the next section, we draw on examples of Federal Reserve lending during the recent crisis to elaborate a bit more on some of these issues.

3. Federal Reserve lending during the crisis

The recent financial crisis marks an important period in recent history in which central banks accumulated a vast amount of experience in the execution of their LOLR role. As highlighted in Domanski et al. (2014), this contrasts sharply with the post-Second World War period, when emergency liquidity support had been provided rarely and almost always to individual banking institutions experiencing idiosyncratic and usually transitory difficulties. In a number of cases, before the recent crisis, central banks had not provided emergency liquidity support for decades.

In this section, to highlight some of the practical issues a central bank faces when making lending decisions, we review some of the liquidity situations that arose during the crisis and that in many instances resulted in lending by the Federal Reserve. First, we describe situations where the Federal Reserve engaged in lending to address a widespread market failure. These cases highlight the kind of liquidity troubles where a LOLR is the best solution and where liquidity regulations would not have been enough—that is, examples that highlight the case reviewed in section 2.1 above. Second, we review situations where the Federal Reserve provided lending to support individual institutions that could possibly have been avoided if these institutions had been subject to liquidity requirements and policymakers had other tools, such as an orderly resolution mechanism. These examples correspond to the type of situation described in section 2.2 and cases where the regulatory tools such as liquidity regulation and a resolution authority may have facilitated better outcomes. In addition, we provide a few examples that highlight the limits a LOLR can face in solving even run-like situations, including cases where the Federal Reserve declined to lend because it was not possible to adequately control or price for credit risk. In doing so, we focus on a few key aspects, including the source of the illiquidity, the riskiness of any loans made (such as indicated by the collateral policies), the level of information the Federal Reserve had about the institutions to which it made the loans, and some discussion about the perceived risks to financial stability should the loans have not been extended.

3.1 Lending in response to marketwide stress

The financial crisis was characterized by the breakdown of several key funding markets. The liquidity needs of financial institutions resulting from those breakdowns were to a significant degree independent of the riskiness of the financial institutions affected. The Federal Reserve's lending during the crisis to address these situations included facilities that can be well classified as lending in response to marketwide problems.

The first example is the breakdown in the market for term interbank funding that occurred at the outset of the crisis. Early in the crisis, troubles in the commercial paper market and in the valuing of structured financial products resulted in banks experiencing liquidity shocks as firms drew down lines of credit and banks brought previously securitized assets back onto their balance sheets that they then needed to fund. In reaction, banks became increasingly reluctant to extend term credit to each other out of fear that they would be short of funding over the term of the prospective interbank loan. Term interbank interest rates rose sharply and the average tenor of interbank borrowing shortened.

In reaction, the Federal Reserve first eased the terms on its main discount window lending program, the primary credit facility (PCF), and later introduced the Term Auction Facility (TAF). In particular, as liquidity of the interbank market deteriorated, the Federal Reserve reduced the spread between the primary credit rate and the target federal funds rate from 100 basis points to 50 basis points on August 17, 2007, then to 25 basis points on March 16, 2008. In addition, the maximum term on these loans was lengthened first from overnight to 30 days and subsequently to as long as 90 days. Despite these changes, during the latter half of 2007, term money market rates persisted at levels well above the primary credit rate, likely because the PCF faced considerable stigma associated with its use. In December 2007, the Federal Reserve introduced the TAF, which auctioned discount window credit to institutions that had access to the PCF. [12] The rate on these loans was determined through an auction process and funds were made available a few days after the auction closed. This facility did not seem to be associated with stigma, possibly because the delay between the auction close and the distribution of funds several days later suggested that the TAF was unlikely to be used by institutions facing imminent funding difficulties and because the auction-determined interest rate was closer to market rates, eliminating any tendency for the bank to appear to have to be "paying up" to receive funding.

---

[12] Prior to the Dodd-Frank Act, information about individual borrowings was not published. However, bankers borrowing from the PCF may have nevertheless feared they would be perceived by their own senior management, supervisors, or counterparties as being unable to obtain funding from normal financial markets at a reasonable price. Armantier et al. (2013) provides some evidence and a helpful discussion of the discount window stigma during the 2007–08 financial crisis.

Use of PCF loans peaked during the crisis at the end of October 2008 at around $110 billion, and lending under the TAF peaked in March 2009 at about $495 billion. The final TAF auction was held on March 8, 2010, with credit extended under that auction maturing on April 8, 2010.[13]

All of these loans—which were extended under the Federal Reserve's regular, not emergency, authority—were generally characterized as low risk to the Federal Reserve or other regulatory and fiscal authorities and made with a considerable amount of knowledge about the counterparties in advance of the loan. The loans were available only to banks in generally sound financial condition, and the institutions able to borrow from this facility were subject to prudential regulations and regularly evaluated by examiners.[14] As a result, the Federal Reserve was relatively confident in the financial health of these banks. In addition, to cover the possibility that the bank defaults and senior creditors are not fully repaid, the Federal Reserve required the borrower to pledge collateral in excess of the amount of the loan. A schedule of haircuts of different types of collateral was published in advance and these haircuts were regularly evaluated to ensure that they would protect the Federal Reserve from losses. Moreover, the Federal Reserve was a senior creditor with full recourse to all the assets of the borrowing bank beyond the collateral. Finally, both programs were clearly designed to provide broad financial stability support rather than to support any specific institution. In the case of the TAF, for example, the institutions receiving the loans were determined through an auction process.

Consistent with the protections in place, these programs appear to have posed little risk to the Federal Reserve ex post, which is especially noteworthy because the crisis took place over many phases, each worse than the preceding one, and each individually worse than anything seen since the Great Depression. The loan balances were often considerably less than the value of the collateral. For example, for TAF loans, the median ratio of loan to available unencumbered collateral at each borrowing bank was 28.6 percent and the 90th percentile of this ratio was 67.8 percent.[15] Of the approximately 2,500 institutions that borrowed from the TAF or PCF

---

[13] See www.federalreserve.gov/newsevents/reform_taf.htm and www.federalreserve.gov/releases/h41.

[14] The primary credit facility is available to depository institutions—banks, credit unions, savings intuitions, and U.S. branches of foreign banks. We use the term "banks" here and elsewhere as short-hand for depository institutions.

[15] See Gilbert et al. (2012) for a discussion of the risk of the loans made under the TAF program.

between July 2007 and the end of 2010, only seven subsequently failed with discount window loans outstanding (in each case, the Federal Reserve was repaid in full).[16]

Another facility that fits well as an example of lending to address marketwide, run-like situations is the Primary Dealer Credit Facility (PDCF), which shares many of the same characteristics of the PCF and TAF. The PDCF provided overnight loans to the primary dealers and was established out of a broader concern about the liquidity situation of other primary dealers at the time when arrangements were being made for J.P. Morgan to acquire Bear Stearns and to avoid a marketwide run. The primary dealers are in many cases subsidiaries of some of the largest financial intermediaries in the United States; maintaining the liquidity of these institutions was seen as important for keeping the financial intermediation process operational. While the Federal Reserve does not supervise these entities and so did not have detailed insights into their financial health, the primary dealers are the institutions with which the Federal Reserve typically conducts monetary policy and has frequent interactions. As such, the Federal Reserve had some familiarity with these institutions. Collateral used to secure loans made through the PDCF was initially limited to investment-grade securities, but in September 2008 was broadened to more closely match the types of instruments that could be pledged in the tri-party repurchase agreement market where dealers typically obtained funding. In addition to the collateral used to secure these loans, PDCF credit was made with recourse beyond the pledged collateral to the primary dealer entity itself, just like PCF lending. Total loans outstanding under the PDCF peaked at around $146 billion on October 1, 2008, and the facility proved itself to be low risk ex post. All the loans were repaid on time with interest. Moreover, the value of the collateral backing the loans remained well above the value of the loans in nearly every instance.[17]

---

[16] Except for one case, the loans at the time of failure were made under the secondary credit program, as the banks had deteriorated so that they no longer qualified for primary credit. Average loan outstanding to these institutions at the time of failure was about $580 million. This average is skewed by one bank with $3 billion in TAF and secondary credit outstanding—the median was $175 million. Five other banks failed during this period with secondary credit loans outstanding, but had not borrowed primary or TAF credit between July 2007 and the end of 2010 and so are not included in this summary.

[17] For example, as of December 17, 2008, the amount of loans outstanding under the PDCF was $47.3 billion. As of the same date, the market value of the collateral pledged under the PDCF was $51.2 billion. ("Periodic Report Pursuant to Section 129(b) of the Emergency Economic Stabilization Act of 2008, Update on Outstanding Lending Facilities Authorized by the Board Under Section 13(3) of the Federal Reserve Act," December 29, 2008.)

3.2 Lending in response to troubles at individual institutions

At the other end of the spectrum of the Federal Reserve's lending were facilities that provided loans to individual institutions suffering liquidity troubles to keep them from defaulting in a disorderly manner. When deciding whether to act, the Federal Reserve had to take into account that the only available resolution mechanism was bankruptcy. There was a concern that the bankruptcy laws would not provide for an orderly resolution of such large complex financial institutions and that these bankruptcies would therefore further disrupt the already severely stressed financial markets to the detriment of the economy as a whole.[18]

The first of these loans was to facilitate the acquisition of Bear Stearns by J.P. Morgan in March 2008. Bear Stearns was a nonbank broker-dealer; in early 2008, market participants became increasingly concerned regarding the firm's solvency and liquidity. Consequently, the firm experienced a run and a rapid depletion of its liquid assets and its ability to meet current obligations. On Thursday, March 13, 2008, Bear Stearns informed the Federal Reserve that it was going to be unable to repay its repurchase agreements and other obligations due the following day. At that time, Bear Stearns was one of the largest securities firms in the United States, and policymakers believed its default would have severely disrupted financial markets, particularly the critical market for repurchase agreements. On Friday, March 14, 2008, to avoid a default by Bear Stearns on that day and to allow time for a more permanent solution to the institution's difficulties, the Federal Reserve lent $12.9 billion to Bear Stearns against $13.8 billion in collateral. On Sunday, March 16, 2008, J.P. Morgan announced that it would purchase Bear Stearns and, to facilitate the acquisition, the Federal Reserve extended a $29 billion non-recourse loan to a limited liability company that it had created and that was on its books called Maiden Lane LLC to acquire about $30 billion of Bear Stearns' less liquid assets.[19] Maiden Lane was also funded by a $1.1 billion subordinated loan from J.P. Morgan that took any initial

---

[18] See Ben Bernanke (2009) "American International Group," testimony before the Committee on Financial Services, U.S. House of Representatives, March 24, www.federalreserve.gov/newsevents/testimony/bernanke20090324a.htm.
[19] See "Report Pursuant to Section 129 of the Emergency Economic Stabilization Act of 2008: Loan to Facilitate the Acquisition of the Bear Stearns Companies, Inc. by JPMorgan Chase & Co."

losses. The loans to Bear Stearns were the first time the Federal Reserve had used its authority to lend to a nonbank since the 1930s.[20]

The second example of a loan made in response to troubles at an individual institution is the one provided to the American International Group (AIG). In early September 2008, concerns about the solvency and liquidity of this institution prompted a run that could have led to fire sales of assets as well as bankruptcy of the institution. As with Bear Stearns, the Federal Reserve judged that the failure of this institution would have caused a massive disruption in financial markets, especially in the wake of the bankruptcy of Lehman Brothers earlier in the week (see below). As such, to prevent the failure of AIG, the Federal Reserve, with the full support of the Treasury, first extended a line of credit for up to $85 billion to assist AIG in meeting its obligations as they came due and to facilitate a process under which AIG would sell certain of its businesses in an orderly manner, with the least possible disruption to the overall economy.[21] The loan had a two-year maturity and was collateralized by a substantial portion of the assets of AIG and its primary nonregulated subsidiaries as well as its equity interest in all of the regulated subsidiaries. Soon thereafter, government support was restructured by the Treasury and the Federal Reserve.[22]

As described by former Chairman Bernanke in his testimony to Congress, "To mitigate concerns that this action would exacerbate moral hazard and encourage inappropriate risk-taking in the future, the Federal Reserve ensured that the terms of the credit extended to AIG imposed significant costs and constraints on the firm's owners, managers, and creditors."[23] Besides the

---

[20] That authority is authorized under section 13(3) of the Federal Reserve Act, and such lending is therefore sometimes called 13(3) lending. Although the Term Securities Loan Facility was authorized on March 11, 2008, it was first used on March 27, after the loan to Bear Stearns.

[21] For details, see "Report Pursuant to Section 129 of the Emergency Economic Stabilization Act of 2008: Secured Credit Facility. Authorized for American International Group, Inc. on September 16, 2008."

[22] The line of credit to AIG was substantially reduced in size and two limited liability companies were established to which the Federal Reserve provided loans to purchase assets from AIG: Maiden Lane II, which purchased illiquid residential real estate assets, and Maiden Lane III, which purchased multi-sector collateralized debt obligations on which AIG had written credit default swaps and other contracts. See reports "Securities Borrowing Facility for American International Group, Inc., on October 6, 2008," "Restructuring of the Government's Financial Support to American International Group, Inc., on November 10, 2008," and "Restructuring of the Government's Financial Support to American International Group, Inc., on March 2, 2009."

[23] See Bernanke, Ben (2008), "U.S. Financial Markets," testimony before the Committee on Banking, Housing, and Urban Affairs, U.S. Senate, September 23, www.federalreserve.gov/newsevents/testimony/bernanke20080923a1.htm#fn1.

collateral for the loan (which comprised all of the assets of the company and its primary non-regulated subsidiaries), the rate charged on the outstanding balance of the loan was three-month Libor plus 850 basis points, implying a current interest rate over 11 percent.[24] In addition, the U.S. government received equity participation rights corresponding to a 79.9 percent equity interest in AIG and had the right to veto the payment of dividends to common and preferred shareholders, among other things.

The key characteristic of these loans is that the risks taken by the Federal Reserve were higher than the risks entailed in the broad-based lending examples mentioned above. In both of these cases, decisions about whether to make the loans needed to be reached very quickly and, while these institutions were judged to be solvent, the Federal Reserve lacked the time to conduct a full assessment to verify that judgment. The Federal Reserve had no supervisory authority over Bear Stearns or AIG and did not have examiners familiar with their operations. For example, Bear Stearns was supervised by the Securities and Exchange Commission, which is primarily concerned with investor protection by promoting the disclosure of important market-related information, maintaining fair dealing, and protecting against fraud. Thus, the Federal Reserve's knowledge about the solvency of Bear Stearns when it was forced to decide whether to make the loan was limited. Moreover, by lending to a special purpose vehicle that acquired specific assets of Bear Stearns, the arrangement capped the possible losses that J.P. Morgan could make on the assets to the amount of its subordinated loan to Maiden Lane and transferred the rest of the risk of the acquired assets to the special purpose vehicle and thus the Federal Reserve.

In addition, as the loans were non-recourse, the Federal Reserve looked exclusively to the value of the collateral to protect itself from losses when making the loans. While the collateral backing the loans consisted of investment-grade securities and performing loans, as the crisis worsened, the fair value of the collateral fell below the amount of the loans from the Federal Reserve at times.[25] For instance, the fair value of the assets in Maiden Lane, at its worst, was about $25 billion, while the loan balance was just over $29 billion in mid-June 2009. But, amid

---

[24] At the time the loan to AIG was restructured, the rate on the line of credit was reduced to three-month Libor plus 300 basis points.

[25] The specific collateral requirements for the loans extended to facilitate the acquisition are described on the New York Fed's website at www.newyorkfed.org/markets/maidenlane.html.

the recovery in financial markets and in the economy more generally, by mid-2010 the value of the assets had increased sufficiently so that it exceeded the value of the loan.[26] All of these loans were fully repaid, with interest, in the end.

3.3 Limits of LOLR

The previous sections illustrate some examples of LOLR loans made to deal with liquidity situations related to market-wide concerns or those related to individual, troubled institutions. In this section, we illustrate the limits and challenges a LOLR faces when responding to crises, which also help point to the value of liquidity regulations and effective resolution mechanisms.

The first example is that of Lehman Brothers, where the Federal Reserve was unable to provide a loan to support the troubled institution. As has been noted in testimony by former Chairman Bernanke, the Federal Reserve understood that the failure of Lehman had the potential to shake the financial system and the economy. However, the only tool available to the Federal Reserve to address the situation was its ability to provide short-term liquidity against adequate collateral, and there was not adequate collateral to back a helpful loan. Lehman needed both substantial capital and an open-ended guarantee of its obligations to continue operating, and at that time neither the Federal Reserve nor any other agency had the authority to provide capital or an unsecured guarantee; thus, no means of preventing Lehman's failure existed.[27] If stronger liquidity regulations had been in place for this institution, in combination with an orderly resolution mechanism, remedial action might have taken place that would have mitigated some of the fallout.

A second example of a challenge faced by the Federal Reserve in providing LOLR loans is one where taking too much collateral might increase the likelihood of a run. During the crisis, investors fled from various institutions or products because the riskiness of those investments had become greater than investors were willing to bear. If the Federal Reserve had fully protected itself when providing loans, it would have increased the risk carried by the remaining

---

[26] "Periodic Report Pursuant to Section 129(b) of the Emergency Economic Stabilization Act of 2008: Update on Outstanding Lending Facilities Authorized by the Board Under Section 13(3) of the Federal Reserve Act, December 29, 2008."June, 2009 and August, 2010.

[27] See Ben Bernanke (2010), "Lessons from the Failure of Lehman Brothers," testimony before the Committee on Financial Services, U.S. House of Representatives, April 10, www.federalreserve.gov/newsevents/testimony/bernanke20100420a.htm.

private investors. Consequently, those remaining investors likely would have rushed to exit as well and the run would have continued or even been exacerbated. Thus, to stop the runs, the Federal Reserve had to be willing to absorb some of the risk. An example that highlights this limitation of a LOLR to solve liquidity problems even in a run-like situation concerns Federal Reserve lending to money market mutual funds (MMMFs) during the crisis. The tidal wave of redemptions from MMMFs after one fund broke the buck in September 2008 because of its Lehman exposures is an example of a modern "bank run." To create a means to contain the run and for MMMFs to liquefy assets without fire sale costs, the Federal Reserve created the Asset-Backed Commercial Paper Money Market Mutual Fund Liquidation Facility (AMLF). The AMLF provided liquidity to MMMFs by extending loans to financial institutions (U.S. depository institutions, bank holding companies, broker-dealers, and branches of foreign banks) that in turn used AMLF loans to purchase highly rated asset-backed commercial paper from MMMFs. To facilitate their intermediary role, the borrowing banks received nonrecourse loans from the AMLF that were collateralized by the asset-backed commercial paper purchased from MMMFs that had no haircuts and could realize a positive spread for acting. The AMLF successfully alleviated the liquidity pressure on the MMMFs, asset-backed commercial paper, and other short-term instruments (Figure 4). Total loans outstanding grew very rapidly, reaching a peak of about $152 billion on October 1, 2008, after just 10 days of operation, and then became sporadic once the redemption pressures ceased.

Shortly after the creation of the AMLF, the Federal Reserve Board approved another facility designed to directly lend to MMMFs—the Direct Money Market Mutual Fund Lending Facility (DMLF)—rather than provide liquidity support through the banks. The DMLF would have allowed the Federal Reserve to make loans that were more similar to its traditional lending through the PCF, with full recourse and positive haircuts applied to the collateral when determining lendable value. However, MMMFs expressed reluctance about borrowing from the Federal Reserve, fearing that investors would recognize that leverage created by a loan would concentrate any losses on the remaining shareholders and increase their incentive to run. Indeed, the industry feared that even opening the facility would be destabilizing. Consequently, the DMLF was never operationalized.[28]

4.   Policy implications

The discussion of the different types of liquidity shocks and the respective policy views in section 2 and the examples of Federal Reserve lending and the challenges it faced during the crisis in section 3 suggest that the optimal policy is a mix of tools, with liquidity and other regulations serving as necessary and beneficial complements to LOLR. In particular, these examples highlight both why liquidity regulations are not sufficient by themselves as well as the potential costs of a LOLR in dealing with liquidity crises. But together, they can help: Liquidity regulations can help reduce the instances in which the central bank is forced to lend to prevent a disorderly failure by discouraging the use of liabilities with higher liquidity risk and by providing time for supervisors to prepare for an orderly default. And central bank lending to address systemic liquidity pressures enables banks to maintain their liquidity reserves to meet idiosyncratic stress and build confidence in the system. In this section, we provide a detailed discussion of these policy implications.

4.1 Liquidity regulations

Liquidity regulations serve both as a tax and a mitigant to help with the externalities associated with liquidity troubles, and also ensure that there's enough liquidity to provide some time to assess and potentially address these troubles without any central bank lending.[29] In particular, liquidity regulations create a tax on liquidity risk-taking by making financial institutions hold a buffer of liquid but low-yielding assets in proportion to their liquidity profile, which should discourage banks from using liabilities that carry the most liquidity risk and also help the bank internalize the social cost of its actions that could result from a severe episode of illiquidity, such

---

[28] See minutes of the meeting of Federal Reserve Board, "Financial Markets—Proposal to Provide Liquidity Directly to Money Market Mutual Funds through the Direct Money Market Mutual Fund Lending Facility," October 3, 2008, pp. 11–12.

[29] For more on this tax and mitigant perspective of liquidity regulations, see Jeremy Stein (2013), "Liquidity Regulation and Central Banking," speech at "Funding the Right Balance," 2013 credit markets wymposium sponsored by the Federal Reserve Bank of Richmond, Charlotte, North Carolina, April 19, www.federalreserve.gov/newsevents/speech/stein20130419a.htm.

as fire sales. Similarly, liquidity regulations, simply by making banks hold greater amounts of liquid assets, ensure that there are more resources to meet margin calls or funding withdrawals, thereby mitigating the need for destabilizing liquidity hoarding and fire sales of assets.

Moreover, Federal Reserve lending experience during the crisis demonstrates that financial authorities need time to respond to a potential default by a large institution so that they can assess the condition of the borrower, determine the extent to which solvency concerns are driving the liquidity need versus marketwide disruptions, and arrange a more orderly and less costly resolution without lending if lending is inappropriate. In these cases, liquidity regulations would ensure that the central bank and the supervisory authority have the necessary time between when a problem is detected and when the default may occur. In this regard, liquidity regulations, like the new liquidity coverage ratio (LCR) requirement, appear well suited. The LCR requires each large bank to hold a sufficient stock of high-quality liquid assets (HQLA) to meet the net cash outflow the bank would experience during 30 days of severe stress. On the assumption that regulatory authorities begin to evaluate the situation of a bank experiencing stress when its LCR falls below 100 percent and that 30 days is sufficient time to either fix the situation or arrange a resolution that is not too socially costly, the LCR should significantly reduce the chances that the Federal Reserve (or other financial authorities) will be forced to lend into a risky situation. Even if liquidity were to vanish faster than envisioned under the LCR, the LCR is still likely to provide some breathing room for the supervisory authorities and the LOLR.

A stockpile of safe and liquid assets potentially has a further advantage. Because of the difficulty of assessing the degree to which solvency issues are driving the liquidity needs of a borrower, it may be impossible for the central bank to be sure that it is charging appropriately for risk if it takes troubled assets as collateral. Using the stockpile as collateral could help ensure any LOLR lending is low risk to the central bank. Put simply, as long as HQLA are readily valued and highly liquid, central bank lending against HQLA could be thought of as a way to liquidate the HQLA rather than as an incidence of LOLR lending. From a moral hazard and cost perspective, the two are equivalent—in either case, the troubled firm liquidates its good assets and pays off its short-term creditors. However, when liquidity issues are affecting multiple institutions in light of a marketwide stress, it is vital that central banks expand the supply of liquid assets. In this circumstance, using the safe and liquid assets as collateral would not accomplish this goal; instead, the LOLR would want to use the least liquid assets as collateral.[30]

Of course, for HQLA to buy time when an institution gets into trouble, they have to be available—they cannot have already been run down. This perspective motivates the "lockbox" view of the liquidity regulations—when an institution uses its liquid assets, the financial authorities should immediately intervene to resolve the situation or the institution. The problem with this approach, however, is that it implies that the banks can't use the liquid assets to help weather a transitory period of illiquidity without supervisory consequences; therefore, banks will hold even more liquid assets than required, which is a potentially undesirable outcome because it reduces lending, increases the odds of fire sales, and adds to the procyclicality of liquidity. Furthermore, for the liquidity regulations to be an effective mitigant against fire sale risk, buffers should be able to be used. The guidance included in the LCR specifies that the ratio can fall below one while at the same time ramping up the policy response. In such circumstances, the supervisors would evaluate and, depending on the degree to which the liquidity situation reflects solvency issues, arrange options for resolving the situation or the institution, and the Federal Reserve would have time to evaluate the options for, and appropriateness of, providing liquidity.

Relatedly, while liquidity regulations should reduce the incidence of central bank lending, the policies should not hamper the ability of central banks to lend to address marketwide liquidity problems. In particular, the regulations—and, perhaps more importantly, the supervision of the regulations—should reduce, not contribute to, stigma associated with borrowing from the central bank.[31] Partly to reduce stigma, the LCR includes an option to recognize committed credit lines from the central bank as a liquid asset, although this option is not used in the United States.

Finally, to minimize LOLR lending to institutions experiencing liquidity issues owing to balance sheet problems, financial institutions that are both funded with runnable liabilities and

---

[30] While imposing a suitable haircut to ensure it is not taking on risk.

[31] Indeed, the Presidents Working Group on Financial Markets and the Financial Stability Forum (since renamed the Financial Stability Board) identified the stigma associated with borrowing from the Federal Reserve's discount window as a significant threat to financial stability. See "Policy Statement on Financial Market Developments," The President's Working Group on Financial Markets, March 2008, p. 9; *Interim Report to the G7 Finance Ministers and Central Bank Governors*, FSF Working Group on Market and Institutional Resilience, April 7, 2008, p. 8; and *Report of the Financial Stability Forum on Enhancing Market and Institutional Resilience*, FSF Working Group on Market and Institutional Resilience, October, 10 2008, p. 35.

are systemically important (either individually or as a group) must be subject to prudential supervision and regulation. Importantly, liquidity and other regulations will be especially necessary for those institutions that are not eligible to borrow from the Federal Reserve. After all, those institutions' failure can still create significant negative externalities for others (for example, by selling assets at fire sale prices as their position deteriorates).

4.2 LOLR policies

While liquidity regulations are a necessary part of the optimal policy mix, they are not a substitute for a LOLR. Requiring banks to hold high enough liquidity buffers to meet liquidity demands associated with a systemic crisis would lead to a less than socially optimal level of liquidity and maturity transformation. More importantly, shortages of liquid assets would be exacerbated during stress episodes as banks would seek to hold larger liquidity buffers on hand and not lend them out as institutions subject to various liquidity shocks become unable to fulfill their obligations in a timely fashion or become concerned about their ability to do so. In other words, banks themselves may not be willing to draw down stockpiles at a time of heightened liquidity concerns. This is a very typical dynamic of liquidity crises historically as discussed in Carlson (2013) and was also evident during the recent crisis. For example, in Figure 5, we plot a summary measure of banks' liquidity (implied liquidity) using quarterly Call Report data for banks with total assets of at least $50 billion and the banks' CAMELS-L rating.[32] The measure is a weighted average of three metrics—liquid assets to total assets, net loans and leases plus standby letters of credit to total assets, and noncore funding to total assets—where the weights are based on the extent to which the metric explains the bank's L rating. These results demonstrate that banks significantly increased their balance sheet liquidity as the crisis unfolded between 2007 and 2009, instead of running down their liquidity buffers.

Accordingly, lending aggressively by the LOLR during times of systemic shocks is a key element of optimal policy to help limit pressures to hoard liquidity and break the procycliality of

---

[32] To create this summary measure, we regress the L rating in the CAMELS rating system on the three liquidity metrics, bank size (measured as log assets), and the ratio of tier 1 capital to assets. The data used in this exercise is a pooled sample of quarterly observations on banks with assets of at least $50 billion during the period from 1995:Q1 to 2006:Q4. Using the coefficients from these regressions we develop a predicted L rating for the crisis years, 2007 through 2009. A lower number for L indicates a better rating so smaller predicted values indicate a shift toward a more liquid balance sheet. We invert the graph so that an upward move in the line is indicative of rising liquidity.

liquidity crises, and even to help support banks' liquidity, keeping the buffers of HQLA in place to withstand inevitable liquidity shocks. In fact, this type of aggressive lending is precisely what is envisioned in the classical doctrine of Bagehot and is also consistent with the Federal Reserve lending to address marketwide disruptions during the crisis. The often repeated catchphrase version of his dictum holds that the central bank should lend freely (that is, without limit) at a penalty rate against good collateral. But, looking at *Lombard Street* more closely highlights the core principles of active lending and using a wide range of collateral that Bagehot explicitly credits with stopping the panic of 1825 (Bagehot, 1873, p. 204):

> The success of the Bank of England on this occasion was owing to its complete adoption of right principles….we [The Bank directors] "lent money by every possible means, and in modes which we had never adopted before; we took in stock on security, we purchased Exchequer Bills, we made advances on Exchequer Bills, we not only discounted outright, but we made advances on deposits of bills of Exchange to an immense amount—in short, by every possible means consistent with the safety of the Bank. . . . and we were not on some occasions over-nice. Seeing the dreadful state in which the public were, we rendered every assistance in our power."

At the same time, a LOLR should not be used to address liquidity situations at individual institutions in which the creditors of an institution pull back out of concern for the riskiness of the institution and its solvency. LOLR lending in these situations cannot be extended in a way that either reliably eliminates or prices correctly for credit risk and so is rife with moral hazard. Lending in these situations is therefore best avoided if at all possible by means of robust liquidity and capital regulations, and means to resolve the institution in an orderly way. One way to eliminate the moral hazard associated with the Federal Reserve being, in effect, forced to lend by the imminent failure of an individual systemically important nonbank is to eliminate the Federal Reserve's authority to lend in such circumstances. In this regard, the Dodd-Frank Act requirement that the Federal Reserve only extend emergency credit through a broad-based facility and not to help an individual troubled institution is a substantial step in that direction. Of course, the shortcoming of this approach is that eliminating the authority to lend does not by itself eliminate the need for such lending. As a result, the restriction increases the importance of the other regulatory changes, especially the development of a credible resolution regime, discussed later.

Perhaps more importantly, while the above reasoning suggests a role for both a LOLR and liquidity regulations, it does not suggest that the appropriate arrangement is for liquidity regulation to stand in front of the LOLR; that is, that a financial institution should first run down its liquidity reserves and only then borrow. Put another way, a LOLR does not seem like the right answer for idiosyncratic situations that are worse than the liquidity stress envisioned in liquidity regulations such as the LCR. If the situation giving rise to the liquidity need is related to concerns about the bank's balance sheet, then the central bank should not lend at all because of the associated credit risk and moral hazard. Instead, the liquidity buffer should be used to provide sufficient time to arrange an orderly resolution (by the institution itself or the authorities) to the underlying problem. On the other hand, if the situation is marketwide, then the LOLR should immediately provide liquidity to address the systemic liquidity pressures so that financial institutions do not need to run down their liquidity buffers, which would further diminish confidence in the institutions. If financial institutions were to instead run down their buffers to meet a systemic liquidity need, the buffers would be depleted in the event an institution had an idiosyncratic problem, consistent with the observation in Tirole (2011): while Goodhart (2008) would argue that liquidity must be usable liquidity, it does not capture the fact that when an institution draws down its liquidity position, it is left exposed to subsequent liquidity shocks that could occur in the near future.

4.3 Resolution authority and other considerations

Another regulatory item that we have alluded to several times in the paper as a tool to reduce the social cost of failure is the importance of adequate resolution procedures, such as the Dodd-Frank Act requirement that the FDIC develop a credible resolution regime for large financial institutions. As we discussed earlier, at times lending to troubled banks by the Federal Reserve was only authorized given the high relative cost of a disorderly failure.

Relatedly, requiring large institutions to maintain a minimum amount of long-term unsecured debt outstanding at the holding company level to capitalize a bridge institution if the institution fails should contribute to a credible resolution regime. Moreover, a requirement for long-term debt could have the benefit of improving market discipline because the holders of that debt would know they faced the prospect of loss should the firm enter resolution.[33] The FDIC's orderly resolution authority includes capacity to provide liquidity to the failed institution as well as a potential guarantee of the institution's short-term debt. The moral hazard associated with this is potentially very similar to that associated with LOLR lending: short-term creditors realize they will not lose money and so do not demand a high rate and do not monitor the riskiness or liquidity of the firm, and the bank will choose to fund itself disproportionately with short-term credit. In sum, it is hard to overcome that moral hazard by credibly planning to make the short-term creditors take losses, so it is important to control the amount of liquidity risk taken. Imposing a long-term credit requirement and planning to recapitalize the banks using the long-term credit gives those creditors a strong incentive to care about the short-term risk of the firm. In that way, the long-term creditors can stand in for the short-term creditors in terms of controlling moral hazard.

Similarly, increasing capital requirements, especially for large, systemically important institutions as was done in the wake of the crisis, is also key to reducing the likelihood of future crises. Increased capital reduces the chance that a financial institution will get into trouble and lead its investors to run; it also reduces the incentive of the owners of the firm to take risks that could result in failure. Lastly, in the event the institution is subject to a random liquidity event, greater capital raises the odds that lending to the institution can be done safely.[34]

For the purposes of reducing the likelihood of lending to troubled institutions, perhaps there should also be a link between capital and liquidity. If an institution exposed to a large amount of potential liquidity risk held more capital, it would be less likely to experience a run, need less liquidity support, and be less likely to need to engage in fire sales that can depress capital levels at the firm and impose externalities on the broader financial system. In this spirit, the recent

---

[33] See Daniel Tarullo (2014), "Dodd-Frank Implementation," testimony before the Committee on Banking, Housing, and Urban Affairs, U.S. Senate, Washington, February 6, www.federalreserve.gov/newsevents/testimony/tarullo20140206a.htm.

[34] See Rochet and Vives (2004) for a formal model illustrating how prompt corrective action and orderly resolution can be used in conjunction with discount window lending to deal with bank runs.

proposal from the Federal Reserve that large institutions' capital requirements be an increasing function of their reliance on short-term wholesale funding would provide just such a link.[35]

5.   Conclusion

The 2007–09 financial crisis was characterized by severe reductions in the liquidity of financial markets, runs on the shadow banking system, and potentially destabilizing defaults and near-defaults of major financial institutions, all of which contributed to a downward spiral as the subsequent curtailment of credit intermediation led to a sharp recession that, in turn, weakened financial institutions further. In response, central banks (primarily the Federal Reserve), in their role as LOLR, injected extraordinary amounts of liquidity. In the aftermath, legislatures and regulators tightened capital and liquidity regulations to reduce the odds that such a crisis would happen again.

In this paper, we argued that both responses—aggressive central bank lending and robust liquidity and other regulations—are necessary and complementary. Aggressive central bank lending is the right response for generalized runs or marketwide deteriorations in liquidity as requiring institutions to hold reserves sufficient to address systemic liquidity episodes would be needlessly costly and probably ineffective. But often illiquidity and insolvency are inexorably intertwined, and robust liquidity reserves buy time for financial institutions to weather periods of illiquidity without government support or for the authorities to arrange orderly resolutions of the institution. Liquidity regulations also lead financial institutions to internalize the externalities associated with the liquidity risk they are undertaking while capital regulations reduce the likelihood that institutions will be insolvent, and both help counter moral hazard.

We illustrated our perspective using examples of the Federal Reserve lending—and, in some cases, *not* lending—during the crisis. In many cases, lending addressed broad-based illiquidity; the fact that all loans were repaid on time with interest supports the view that lending entailed relatively low risk, especially considering the increasing severity of the crisis as it unfolded. In

---

[35] See Board of Governors of the Federal Reserve System (2014), "Federal Reserve Board Proposes Rule to Further Strengthen the Capital Positions of the Largest, Most Systemically Important U.S. Bank Holding Companies," press release, December 9, www.federalreserve.gov/newsevents/press/bcreg/20141209a.htm.

other cases, though—primarily when specific institutions whose failure would have significantly worsened the crisis came under pressure—the Federal Reserve had to respond quickly and made loans that, while collateralized, appear to have been riskier than other loans extended during the crisis.

We then reviewed the implications of our analysis for financial regulation and central bank lending. In sum, the suite of post-crisis liquidity and capital regulations appears likely to reduce the incidence of future crises in part by causing financial institutions to internalize the externalities associated with illiquidity. But, it will be important that the regulatory and supervisory response recognize and not hamper the important role of LOLR lending in response to a financial crisis. Indeed, a forceful response by the central bank is the optimal response to broad-based episodes of illiquidity. Moreover, it is not correct to think of the liquidity buffers of institutions as something always to be used as a line of first defense before central bank lending. Liquidity buffers and a LOLR serve different purposes: in some cases, such as during a systemic shock, it is optimal to respond right away with central bank lending; in other situations, such as during idiosyncratic shocks at individual institutions, it is optimal to run down the buffers and have the supervisory authorities intervene as needed. We also note that while central banks can to some extent control the potential moral hazard associated with lending by pricing credit risk correctly or, more practically, by driving credit risk to zero by taking on lots of collateral, this approach may actually hinder their ability to address liquidity troubles at times. Consequently, it will also be important to establish sufficiently low-cost resolution regimes to reduce the cost of allowing an institution to fail, and that institutions be allowed to fail—rather than lent to by a LOLR—when their illiquidity is the consequence of solvency rather than liquidity concerns.

References

Acharya, Viral V., Denis Gromb, and Tanju Yorulmazer (2012). "Imperfect Competition in the Interbank Market for Liquidity as a Rationale for Central Banking," *American Economic Journal: Macroeconomics*, vol. 4 (2), pp. 184–217.

Allen, Franklin, and Douglas Gale (2007). *Understanding Financial Crises*. Oxford: Oxford University Press.

Armantier, Olivier, Eric Ghysels, Asani Sarkar, and Jeffrey Shrader (2013). *Discount Window Stigma during the 2007-2008 Financial Crisis*, Staff Report 483. New York: Federal Reserve Bank of New York, September.

Bagehot, Walter (1873). *Lombard Street, A Description of the Money Market*. Reprint. New York: Charles Scribner and Sons, 1909.

Bindseil, Ulrich (2013). "Central Bank Collateral, Asset Fire Sales, Regulation and Liquidity," European Central Bank Working Paper Series 1610 (Frankfurt: European Central Bank, November).

Board of Governors of the Federal Reserve System (1971). *Reappraisal of the Federal Reserve Discount Mechanism* (Washington: Board of Governors).

Bordo, Michael D. (1990). "The Lender of Last Resort: Alternative Views and Historical Experience," Federal Reserve Bank of Richmond, *Economic Review*, January/February, pp. 18–29.

Buiter, Willem (2007). "What Did You Do in the Open Market Today, Daddy?," *Financial Times: Maverecon Blog*, December 13, http://blogs.ft.com/maverecon/2007/12/what-did-you-dohtml/#axzz30yQL97u0.

Calomiris, Charles (1994). "Is the Discount Window Necessary? A Penn Central Perspective," *Federal Reserve Bank of St. Louis Review*, vol. 76 (3), pp. 31–55.

Campbell, Sean, Daniel Covitz, William Nelson, and Karen Pence (2011). "Securitization Markets and Central Banking: An Evaluation of the Term Asset-Backed Securities Loan Facility," *Journal of Monetary Economics*, vol. 58 (5), pp. 518–31.

Cao, Jin, and Gerhald Illing (2011). "Endogenous Exposure to Systemic Liquidity Risk," *International Journal of Central Banking*, vol. 7 (2), pp. 173–216.

Carlson, Mark (2013). "Lessons from the Historical Use of Reserve Requirements in the United States to Promote Bank Liquidity," Finance and Economics Discussion Series 2013-11. Washington: Board of Governors of the Federal Reserve System, January).

Carlson, Mark, and David Wheelock (2012). "The Lender of Last Resort: Lessons from the Fed's First 100 Years," Working Paper Series 2012-056. (St. Louis: Federal Reserve Bank of St. Louis, November).

Corrigan, E. Gerald (1990). "Statement by E. Gerald Corrigan, President, Federal Reserve Bank of New York, with Appendices," statement before the Subcommittee on Domestic Monetary Policy of the Committee on Banking, Finance, and Urban Affairs, U.S. House of Representatives, December 12.

Diamond, Douglas, and Philip Dybvig (1983). "Bank Runs, Deposit Insurance, and Liquidity," *Journal of Political Economy,* vol. 91 (3), pp. 401–19.

Domanski, Dietrich, Richhild Moessner, and William R. Nelson (2014). "Central Banks as Lender of Last Resort: Experiences during the 2007–2010 Crisis and Lessons for the Future," BIS Papers 79 (September), pp. 76–80.

Duygan-Bump, Burcu, Patrick Parkinson, Eric Rosengren, Gustavo A. Suarez, and Paul Willen (2013). "How Effective Were the Federal Reserve Emergency Liquidity Facilities? Evidence from the Asset-Backed Commercial Paper Money Market Mutual Fund Liquidity Facility," *Journal of Finance*, vol. 68 (2), pp. 715–37.

Farhi, Emmanuel, and Jean Tirole (2012). "Collective Moral Hazard, Maturity Mismatch and Systemic Bailouts," *American Economic Review*, vol. 102 (1), pp. 60–93.

Federal Deposit Insurance Corporation (1997), *History of the Eighties—Lessons for the Future* Chap. 7: Continental Illinois and Too Big to Fail, pp. 235–257. Washington: Federal Deposit Insurance Corporation, www.fdic.gov/bank/historical/history.

Freixas, Xavier (1999). "Optimal Bail-Out, Conditionality, and Creative Ambiguity," CEPR Discussion Papers 2238. United Kingdom: Centre for Economic Policy Research.

Freixas, Xavier, Curzio Giannini, Glenn Hoggarth, and Farouk Soussa (1999). "Lender of Last Resort: A Review of the Literature," *Financial Stability Review* (November), pp. 151–67.

Freixas, Xavier, Curzio Giannini, Glenn Hoggarth, and Farouk Soussa (2000). "Lender of Last Resort: What Have We Learned Since Bagehot?" *Journal of Financial Services Research*, vol. 19 (1), pp. 63–84.

Friedman, Milton, and Anna Schwartz (1963). *A Monetary History of the United States, 1867–1960*. Princeton, NJ: Princeton University Press.

Gilbert, R. Alton, Kevin Kliesen, Andrew Meyer, and David Wheelock (2012). "Federal Reserve Lending to Troubled Banks during the Financial Crisis, 2007–2010," *Federal Reserve Bank of St. Louis Review*, vol. 94 (May/June), pp. 221–42.

Goodfriend, Marvin (2011). "Central Banking in the Credit Turmoil: An Assessment of Federal Reserve Practice," *Journal of Monetary Economics,* vol. 58 (January), pp. 1–12.

Goodfriend, Marvin, and Robert King (1988). "Financial Deregulation, Monetary Policy, and Central Banking," in W. Haraf and R. Kushmeider, eds., *Restructuring Banking and Financial Services in America*. Washington: American Enterprise Institute, pp. 216–53.

Goodhart, Charles (1985). *The Evolution of Central Banks*. London: London School of Economics and Political Science.

Goodhart, Charles (1987). "Why Do Banks Need a Central Bank?" *Oxford Economic Papers*, vol. 39 (March), pp. 75–89.

Goodhart, Charles (1999). "Myths about the Lender of Last Resort," *International Finance*, vol. 2 (3), 339–60.

Goodhart, Charles (2008). "Liquidity Risk Management," Banque de France, *Financial Stability Review*, vol. 11 (February), pp. 39–44.

Goodhart, Charles, and Dirk Schoenmaker (1995). "Institutional Separation between Supervisory and Monetary Agencies," in Charles Goodhart, ed., *The Central Bank and the Financial System.* Cambridge, MA: MIT Press, pp. 333–413.

Gorton, Gary, and Andrew Metrick (2013). "The Federal Reserve and Panic Prevention: The Roles of Financial Regulation and Lender of Last Resort," *Journal of Economic Perspectives*, vol. 27 (4), pp. 45–64.

Gorton, Gary, and George Pennacchi (1990), "Financial Intermediaries and Liquidity Creation," *Journal of Finance,* vol. 45 (March), pp. 49–71.

Holmstrom, Bengt, and Jean Tirole (1998). "Private and Public Supply of Liquidity," *Journal of Political Economy,* vol. 106 (1), pp. 1–40.

Kashyap, Anil K., Raghuram Rajan, and Jeremy C. Stein (2002), "Banks as Liquidity Providers: An Explanation for the Coexistence of Lending and Deposit-Taking," *Journal of Finance,* vol. 57 (February), pp. 33–73.

Lacker, Jeffrey (2012). "A Program for Financial Stability," speech delivered at the Banking Institute, UNC School of Law, Charlotte, NC, March 29.

Riksbank (2003). "The Riksbank's Role as Lender of Last Resort," *Financial Stability Report*, vol. 2, pp. 57–73.

Rochet, Jean-Charles, and Xavier Vives (2004). "Coordination Failures and the Lender of Last Resort: Was Bagehot Right After All?" *Journal of the European Economic Association,* vol. 2 (6), pp. 1116–47.

Rochet, Jean-Charles, and Jean Tirole (1996). "Interbank Lending and Systemic Risk," *Journal of Money, Credit and Banking*, vol. 28 (4), pp. 733–62.

Rosengren, Eric (2012). "Money Market Mutual Funds and Financial Stability," remarks at the 2012 Financial Markets Conference sponsored by the Federal Reserve Bank of Atlanta, held in Stone Mountain, Georgia, April 11.

Schwartz, Anna J. (1992). "The Misuse of the Fed's Discount Window," *Federal Reserve Bank of St. Louis Review*, vol. 74 (September/October), pp. 58–69.

Schwartz, Anna J. (1995). "Coping with Financial Fragility," *Journal of Financial Services Research,* vol. 9 (3), pp. 445–51.

Sprague, O.M.W. (1913). *Banking Reform in the United States.* Cambridge, MA: Harvard University Press.

Stern, Gary, and Ron Feldman (2004). *Too Big to Fail: The Hazards of Bank Bailouts.* Washington: Brookings Institution Press.

Tirole, Jean (2011). "Illiquidity and All Its Friends," *Journal of Economic Literature*, vol. 49 (2), pp. 287–325.

Thornton, Henry (1802). *An Enquiry into the Nature and Effects of the Paper Credit of Great Britain.* London: J. Hatchard, Bookseller to the Queen.

Volcker, Paul (1985). "Statement by Paul Volcker, Chairman, Federal Reserve" statement before the Subcommittee on Domestic Monetary Policy of the Committee on Banking, Finance, and Urban Affairs, U.S. House of Representatives, December 12.

Figure 1: Three-month Libor-OIS spread, July 2007–July 2009

Photo Removed Due to Copyright Restrictions

Source: Bloomberg Finance, L.P.

Figure 2: Selected assets of the Federal Reserve, August 2007–August 2010

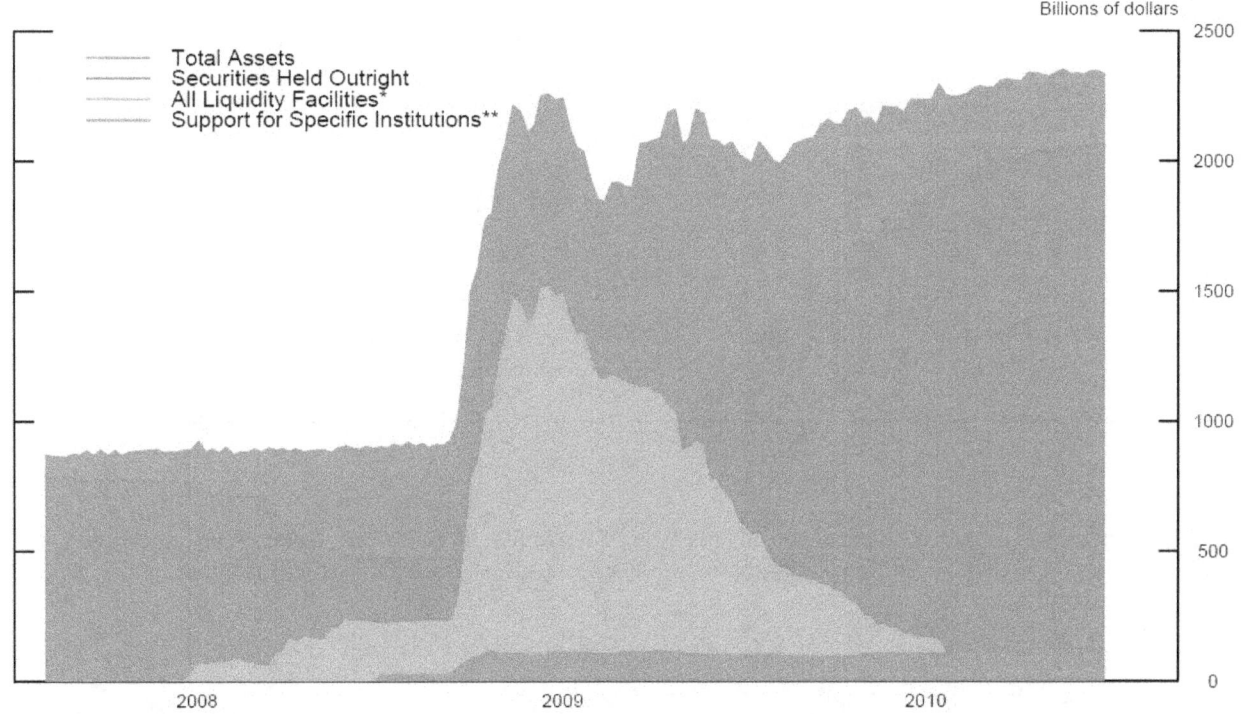

Billions of dollars

Total Assets
Securities Held Outright
All Liquidity Facilities*
Support for Specific Institutions**

2500

2000

1500

1000

500

0

2008   2009   2010

* "All Liquidity Facilities" includes Term Auction credit, primary credit, secondary credit, seasonal credit, Primary Dealer Credit Facility, Asset-Backed Commercial Paper Money Market Mutual Fund Liquidity Facility, Term Asset-Backed Securities Loan Facility, Commercial Paper Funding Facility, and central bank liquidity swaps.
** "Support for Specific Institutions" includes Maiden Lane LLC, Maiden Lane II LLC, Maiden Lane III LLC, and support to AIG.
*** "Support to AIG" includes credit extended to American International Group as well as preferred interests in AIA Aurora LLC and ALICO Holdings LLC.
Source: Board of Governors of the Federal Reserve System, Statistical Release H.4.1, "Factors Affecting Reserve Balances, www/federalreserve.gov/releases/h41.

Figure 3: Money market mutual fund assets, July–December 2008

Photo Removed Due to Copyright Restrictions

Source: Investment Company Institute.

Figure 4: Spreads on overnight commercial paper, July 2007 – July 2009

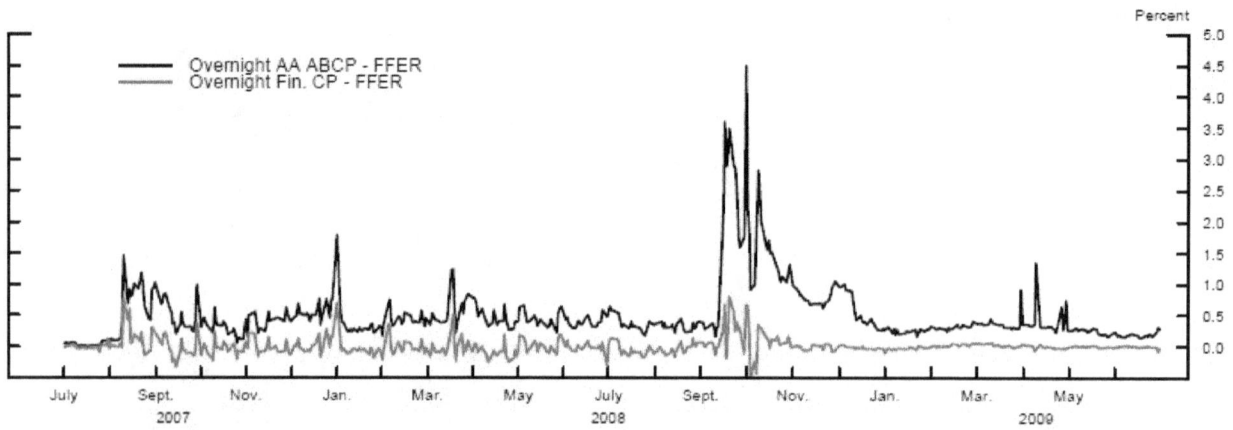

Note: Daily overnight commercial paper spreads over the effective federal funds rate, based on at-issue yields.
Source: Federal Reserve, derived from data supplied by The Depository Trust & Clearing Corporation.

Figure 5: Evolution of implied liquidity at large banks, 2007-09

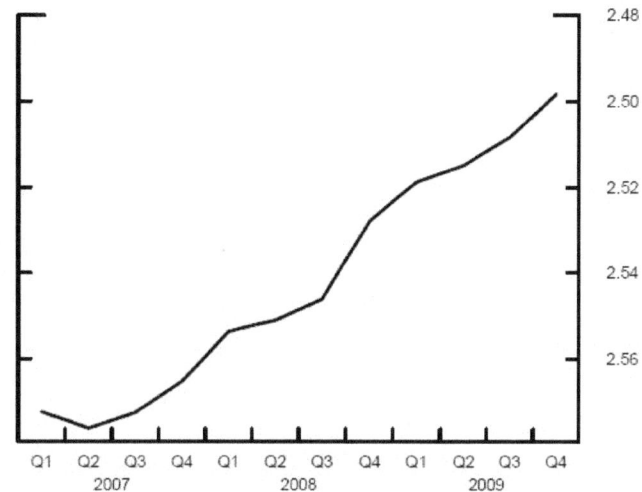

Note: "Implied liquidity" is a summary measure of liquidity constructed using CAMELS L ratings and quarterly Call Report data from a sample of large banks, defined as banks with at least $50 billion in total assets. Note that because this summary is constructed using the regulatory liquidity rating L in CAMELS ratings, a lower number indicates a stronger liquidity position. We invert the graph so that an upward move in the line is indicative of rising liquidity.
Source: Authors' calculations based on quarterly Capp Report data and CAMELS L ratings.